Southern Comfort Cooking: 25 Authentic and Delicious Recipes from Down South

Disclaimer and Terms of Use: Effort has been made to ensure that the information in this book is accurate and complete, however, the author and the publisher do not warrant the accuracy of the information, text and graphics contained within the book due to the rapidly changing nature of science, research, known and unknown facts and Internet. The Author and the publisher do not hold any responsibility for errors, omissions or contrary interpretation of the subject matter herein. This book is presented solely for motivational and informational purposes only.

Table of Contents

Southern Style Biscuits

Serves: 8 to 12
Cooking Time: 30 minutes

Ingredients

4 cups flour, rising
1 tbsp baking powder
1 tbsp sugar
¾ cup shortening, vegetable
2 cups buttermilk

Directions

I.   Preheat the oven to 400 °F and spray the baking sheet with nonstick spray.
II.   In a large mixing bowl, combine all of the ingredients and mix well.
III.   Using a pastry cutter or a fork, cut the shortening into the dough until crumbly.
IV.   Add buttermilk and stir until the dough is soft.
V.   Sprinkle a surface with flour and roll out the dough using a cookie cutter or something rough (a lid from a mason jar works great).
VI.   Cut out biscuits from the dough and place on the baking sheet.
VII.   Bake for 10 to 12 minutes or until golden brown.
VIII. Serve warm.

Nutritional Information

Calories 178, Fat 4.7g, Carbs 28.9g, Protein 2.9g

Cheesy Bread

Serves: 8 to 20
Cooking Time: 1 hour

Ingredients

1/2 cup cornmeal, white
1 cup water, boiling
2 tbsp butter
1 1/2 tsp baking powder
1/2 tsp salt and pepper
3 eggs
1/2 cup milk
1 can chilies, green, chopped and drained
1 cup Mexican-blend cheese, shredded

Directions

I.   Preheat oven to 400 °F and grease a large loaf pan.
II.   In a medium to large-size mixing bowl, blend the first six ingredients.
III.   Once it is mixed well, blend in the eggs and milk and beat for 1 to 2 minutes longer.
IV.   Pour half of the batter into the greased loaf pan and spoon the chilies over the top of the dough. Add 2/3 cup cheese and pour remaining 1/2 of the batter over the top of the cheese and chilies.
V.   Top off with the rest of the cheese and chilies.
VI.   Bake uncovered for 20 to 25 minutes or until golden brown.
VII.   Serve warm.

Nutritional Information

Calories 171, Fat 2.2g, Carbs 29.7g, Protein 5.4g

Serves: 12
Cooking Time: 30 to 45 minutes

Ingredients

1 1/2 cups milk

1/3 cup oil, vegetable

1 egg

2 cups cornmeal, yellow

1 cup flour

3 tbsp sugar

1 tbsp baking powder

1 tsp salt

Directions

I. Preheat the oven to 425 °F and grease the muffin tin with cooking spray.
II. Add all of the ingredients to a mixing bowl and mix well.
III. One everything is completely combined, spoon the dough into each of the muffin tins.
IV. Bake for 16 to 20 minutes.
V. Remove from oven and let them cool before serving.

Nutritional Information

Calories 149, Fat: 5.8g, Carbs 18.6g, Protein 4g

Serves: 6
Cooking Time: 20 minutes

Ingredients

3 1/2 cups water
1 cup grits, white
1 cup cheese, cheddar, shredded
4 tbsp butter
1/4 cup milk
1/2 tsp salt and pepper
1/8 tsp pepper, red, ground

Directions

I. Bring the water to a boil in a large saucepan and add the grits, cook for about 5 to 7 minutes, stir every few seconds until the mix thickens.
II. Remove from the heat after 7 minutes and add the cheese and butter, stir until both are melted.
III. Add in the rest of the ingredients and stir so that everything is well blended.
IV. Serve right away or you can store in fridge, covered, and reheat to serve.

Nutritional Information

Calories 235, Fat 12.7g, Carbs 15g, Protein 14.7g

Serves: 6
Cooking Time: 25 to 30 minutes

Ingredients

1 egg
¼ cup water
1 ½ tsp salt and pepper to taste
5 green tomatoes, cored and sliced
1 cup flour
1 cup self-rising cornmeal mix
1 ½ cup vegetable oil

Directions

I.   In a large mixing bowl, combine the eggs, water, salt and pepper and stir really well. Once it is well blended, stir in the tomatoes in small batches of slices.

II.   In a separate dish, add the cornmeal and flour and mix well. Dip the tomato slices into the flour mix and be sure to cover completely.

III.   In a skillet, heat the oil. Once it is hot, fry the tomatoes for about 2 minutes on each side. Once golden brown, remove from the heat and add to a plate with a paper towel to absorb the excess grease.

Nutritional Information

Calories 181, Fat 2g, Carbs 38.6g, Protein 4.6g

Southern Baked Beans

Serves: 8
Cooking Time: 4 hours

Ingredients

   1/2 lb ground beef, ground
   1/2 cup onion, chopped
   1 1/2 cup barbecue sauce
   1/3 cup sugar, brown
   1/2 cup water
   1 can kidney beans, drained
   1 can butter beans, drained
   1 can pork and beans, drained
   1/2 cup bacon, crumbs

Directions

I.   Add the meat, onion, sauce, sugar and water to a slow cooker and stir well. Once all of it is well blended, go ahead and stir in the rest of the ingredients.

II.   Cover the slow cooker and cook on high for 4 hours.

Nutritional Information

   Calories 234, Fat 9.1g, Carbs 39.1g, Protein 6.1g

Serves: 10
Cooking Time: 30 minutes

Ingredients

1 cup mayo
3 tbsp lemon juice
2 tbsp sugar
1 tsp salt
6 cups cabbage, shredded
1 cup carrots, shredded
½ cup peppers, green, chopped

Directions

I.   Use a large mixing bowl and combine all of the ingredients, stir well.
II.   Once everything is in the bowl and has been stirred, lightly toss as well to make sure it is well coated.
III.   Chill and serve.

Nutritional Information

Calories 64, Fat 2.9g, Carbs 8g, Protein 2.6g

Fried Okra

Serves: 4
Cooking Time: 20 minutes

Ingredients

1/4 cup flour
1/2 cup cornmeal, yellow
1/8 tsp pepper, cayenne
1 1/2 tsp salt
1 lb okra, trimmed and sliced
2 cups oil, vegetable

Directions

I.   Add the flour, cornmeal, salt and cayenne pepper to a Ziploc® bag, seal and toss or shake well to blend everything together.
II. Rinse and slice the okras and add them to the bag, seal and shake. Coat them completely.
III. Add the oil to the skillet and cook the okra for about 3 to 4 minutes on each side. Remove from the skillet to a paper towel lined plate to soak up excess grease.
IV. Cook the remaining okra until they are all done and season to taste.

Nutritional Information

Calories 198, Fat 14.1g, Carbs 16.2g, Protein 4.1g

Serves: 3
Cooking Time: 30 minutes

Ingredients

3 tsp chili powder
1 tsp salt
¼ tsp pepper
6 sweet potatoes, peeled, sliced into fries or wedges

Directions

I.   Preheat oven to 425 °F and spray the cookie sheet with nonstick spray.

II.   In a large Ziploc® baggie, add the seasonings and chili powder.

III.   Add the potato fries or wedges, seal bag and shake to coat.

IV.   Lay the potatoes out on the cookie sheet in a single layer and bake for 20 to 25 minutes. The potatoes should be tender and a golden color.

Nutritional Information

Calories 117, Fat 5.4g, Carbs 16.4g, Protein 1.2g

Southern Style Green Beans

Serves: 6
Cooking Time: 10 to 15 minutes

Ingredients

2 tbsp butter
1/2 cup tomatoes, sun dried
1/3 cup walnuts, chopped
2 tbsp garlic, minced
3 packages green beans, Italian
3/4 tsp salt

Directions

I.   Melt the butter over medium heat in a medium-to-large skillet.
II.   Add in everything but the green beans and sauté lightly for about one minute.
III.   After the minute, stir in the green beans, season with salt and sauté for about 5 to 6 minutes until everything is soft and tender.

Nutritional Information

Calories 403, Fat 17.5g, Carbs 18.5g, Protein 30.5g

Serves: 4
Cooking Time: 1 hour and 15 minutes

Ingredients

2 lbs chicken, drumsticks
½ tsp salt and pepper to taste
1 cup BBQ sauce
1 tsp hot pepper sauce
2 tsp oregano, dried
2 tsp cumin

Directions

I.   Preheat the oven to 375 °F and grease the baking dish with butter or nonstick spray.
II.   Add the drumsticks to the dish and season to taste with salt and pepper.
III.   Bake the chicken for about 30 minutes.
IV.   In a small mixing bowl, combine the rest of the ingredients and stir well.
V.   Pour the sauce over the chicken in the baking dish and cook the chicken for another 30 to 45 minutes. The chicken is cooked when the juices run clear. You do not want any pink juice.

Nutritional Information

Calories 94, Fat 1.3g, Carbs 12g, Protein 7.6g

Serves: 6
Cooking Time: 6 hours and 30 minutes

Ingredients

3 1/3 to 4 lbs pork roast
1/4 tsp salt and pepper
1/2 tsp garlic powder
1 tbsp oil, vegetable
1/4 cup wine, white
1 package mushrooms, sliced
1 onion, chopped
1 can soup, cream of mushroom
1/4 cup sour cream
2 tbsp mustard, Dijon

Directions

I.   Season the pork with all of the seasonings listed and brown along the edges. Go all the way around in the skillet for about 5 minutes.
II.   In a slow cooker, add the remaining ingredients and stir well.
III.   Add the seasoned pork roast and spoon the juices/sauce over the meat.
IV.   Cover and cook for 6 to 8 hours on low or until the meat is tender.

Nutritional Information

Calories 439, Fat 31.8g, Carbs 4.7g, Protein 31.8g

Serves: 4
Cooking Time: 25 to 30 minutes

Ingredients

4 6 oz catfish, fillets
1 cup cheese, Parmesan, grated
½ stick butter
3 scallions, sliced
½ tsp Worcestershire sauce
½ tsp hot sauce
½ cup mayo

Directions

I. Preheat the oven to 350 °F and coat the baking sheet with a cooking spray.
II. In a mixing bowl, combine everything but the catfish, make sure it is well blended.
III. Lay the fish on the baking sheet and spread or pour the mix over the fish.
IV. Bake for 20 to 25 minutes until the fish is a golden color.

Nutritional Information

Calories 198, Fat 10.6g, Carbs 5.7g, Protein 19.2g

Serves: 3 to 4
Cooking Time: 20 to 30 minutes

Ingredients

½ cup milk
1 egg
1 chicken, cut up
1 cup flour
1 tbsp salt and pepper to taste
3 cup oil, vegetable

Directions

I.   Blend the milk and egg in a large mixing bowl and whisk well.
II.   Add the chicken to the bowl and coat thoroughly.
III.   In a separate mixing bowl, add the dry ingredients.
IV.   Dip the chicken in the dry ingredients, coating everything.
V.   Heat the oil in a large, deep skillet. Once the oil is bubbling, not smoking, add a few pieces of the chicken at a time. Flip the chicken and cook on both sides, frying all the way around.
VI.   Cooking time is about 20 to 25 minutes.
VII.   Add the chicken to a paper towel lined plate to absorb excess grease.

Nutritional Information

Calories 301, Fat 2.6g, Carbs 12.6g, Protein 27.3g

Serves: 6
Cooking Time: 1 hour

Ingredients

1 lb shrimp, large, peeled and prepared
1 lb fish filets, chopped and chunked
1 piece pork, salted, skinless and chopped
2 onions, chopped
1 can tomatoes, drained and halved
1 can tomato sauce
1 can tomato paste
2 tbsp Worcestershire sauce
½ tsp black pepper, cracked

Directions

I. Using a large stockpot, cook the salted pork for a few minutes. It should be a golden brown color.
II. Add the onions and sauté until they are soft and tender, almost translucent.
III. Stir in the tomatoes with the liquid, sauce, paste, Worcestershire and pepper. Bring everything to a boil in the stockpot, then add in the fish and shrimp.
IV. Reduce to a simmer and cook for about 25 to 20 minutes. Watch for the soup to thicken and the fish to be cooked.

Nutritional Information

Calories 221, Fat 8.9g, Carbs 16.8g, Protein 19.1g

Homestyle Chicken Fried Steak

Serves: 4
Cooking Time: 10 to 15 minutes

Ingredients

4 steaks, cube
1 tsp salt and pepper to taste
¾ cup buttermilk
¾ cup cornmeal
½ cup shortening, vegetable
3 tbsp flour
1 ½ cup milk

Directions

I. Season the cube steaks with salt and pepper and set aside.
II. Add the buttermilk in one dish and the cornmeal in a separate dish. Lay side by side and dip the steaks in the buttermilk first, then the cornmeal and make sure the steaks are well coated.
III. Heat the shortening in the skillet. Once it is hot and melted, add the steaks and cook for about 4 to 5 minutes per side. Cook each side thoroughly. After they are cooked, add steaks to a paper towel lined plate to absorb the excess grease.
IV. Add the remaining flour, salt and pepper to the skillet, cook until the flour is browned and be sure to constantly stir.
V. Add in the milk and stir until the sauce thickens.
VI. Serve gravy over the top of the chicken fried steaks.

Nutritional Information

Calories 302, Fat 15.4g, Carbs 15.7g, Protein 25.8g

Cajun Steak

Serves: 2 to 4
Cooking Time: 25 to 30 minutes

Ingredients

2 tsp salt
1 tsp pepper
¼ tsp pepper, cayenne
¼ tsp paprika
¼ tsp garlic powder
steaks, beef sirloin

Directions

I.   Preheat the broiler.
II.   In a small mixing bowl, combine all the ingredients except the steak.
III.   Once the seasonings are well blended, rub them on both sides of steaks.
IV.   Add the steaks to the broiler pan or baking sheet that is coated with nonstick spray.
V.   Broil for 6 to 8 minutes on each side for medium rare. Cook longer if desired.

Nutritional Information

Calories 401, Fat 13.6g, Carbs 32.3g, Protein 51.7g

Country Apple Crisp

Serves: 8
Cooking Time: 1 hour

Ingredients

2 cups stuffing, cornbread
1/2 cup butter, melted
orange zest
1 cup pecans, chopped
1/2 tsp cinnamon
1/2 tsp nutmeg
1 cup sugar
8 apples, granny smith, cored, peeled, sliced
1/2 cup water

Directions

I.   Preheat the oven to 350 °F.
II.   In a mixing bowl, blend the stuffing, butter, zest, nuts, spices and 1/2 cup sugar.
III.   In a separate mixing bowl, add the sliced apples and 2/3 cup of the sugar and water.
IV.   Pour the apple mix into the baking dish and top with the crumb mixture. Cover the apples completely and evenly.
V.   Bake for 40 to 45 minutes. The apples should be tender and warm and the juices should be bubbling.

Nutritional Information

Calories 172, Fat 6.4g, Carbs 42.9g, Protein 3.4g

Coconut Cake

Serves: 12
Cooking Time: 25 to 30 minutes

Ingredients

1 package cake mix, white
1 cup water
½ cup milk, coconut, divided
¼ cup oil, vegetable
2 eggs
1 container cool whip, frozen, but thawed
coconut flakes

Directions

I.   Preheat the oven to 350 °F.
II.   Grease round cake pans and set aside.
III.   In a large mixing bowl and using a mixer for about 2 minutes, mix the cake mix, water, ¼ cup coconut milk, oil and eggs with the mixer.
IV.   Pour the batter into two round cake pans.
V.   Bake for 25 to 30 minutes, remove from the oven and let cool. To check that it is cooked thoroughly, stick a toothpick in the center. When it comes out clear, it is done.
VI.   Remove the cakes from pans and cool on a top wire rack. Poke holes into the bottom of the cakes.
VII.   Pour the remaining ¼ cup coconut milk over the cake on a serving plate.
VIII.   Frost the top with whipped cream and add coconut flakes. Add a second layer over the top and repeat with whipped cream and coconut flakes.
IX.   Serve chilled.

Nutritional Information

Calories 226, Fat 11g, Carbs 29.5g, Protein 2.1g

Serves: 24
Cooking Time: 1 hour and 20 minutes

Ingredients

3 eggs
1 ½ cup + 3 tbsp sugar
¾ cup oil, vegetable
¼ cup orange juice
1 tsp vanilla extract
3 cup flour
3 tsp baking powder
1 can pie filling, cherry
1 tsp cinnamon

Directions

I.   Preheat the oven to 350 °F.
II.   Greasing the baking dish.
III.   In a large mixing bowl, cream the eggs, 1 ½ cup sugar, oil, juice and vanilla.
IV.   Stir in the dry ingredients, flour and baking powder, and mix well.
V.   Pour half of the cake batter into the baking dish and pour the pie filling over the batter.
VI.   In a smaller mixing bowl, mix the remaining sugar and cinnamon.
VII.   Pour the rest of the batter over the pie filling.
VIII. Spoon the rest of the batter over the pie filling.
IX.   Bake for 15 minutes, reduce heat to 300 °F and bake for 1 hour.
X.   Remove from oven when a toothpick inserted in it comes out clean.

Nutritional Information

Calories 201, Fat 7.4g, Carbs 31.1g, Protein 3.4g

Pecan Pie

Serves: 8
Cooking Time: 45 to 55 minutes

Ingredients

1 cup corn syrup, light
3 tbsp butter
½ cup sugar, brown, packed
2 tbsp flour
¼ tsp salt
3 eggs, whisked
1 ½ tsp vanilla
1 ½ cup pecans, chopped
1 pie crust, ready-to-bake

Directions

I. Preheat the oven to 350 °F.
II. Heat syrup, butter, sugar, salt and nuts in a skillet and cook until the butter melts.
III. Remove the skillet from the heat and add in the eggs and vanilla, sir well. Stir in the pecans and pour into the premade shell.
IV. Bake the pie for about one hour. Watch for the pie to firm up.
V. Serve warm.

Nutritional Information

Calories 486, Fat 24.4g, Carbs 62.6g, Protein 6.9g

Southern Sunset Red Velvet Cake

Serves: 12
Cooking Time: 35 to 45 minutes

Ingredients

1 package cake mix, yellow or butter

¼ cup cocoa

¾ cup butter, softened

1 cup water

3 eggs

1 oz food coloring, red

1 ½ cup sugar, powdered

1 package cream cheese, softened

1 tbsp milk

Directions

I. Preheat the oven to 350 °F and coat two round cake pans with nonstick spray or shortening and flour.

II. In a mixing bowl and using a mixer, beat the cake mix, coca, ½ cup butter, water and eggs.

III. Once it is well blended, add in the food coloring and beat until well blended.

IV. Pour the batter into prepared cake pans.

V. Bake for about 35 to 40 minutes.

VI. Let it cool for about 10 to 15 minutes before frosting.

VII. Once it is cool, use a long knife and slice cake horizontally. You will now have four sheets.

VIII. Make the frosting by mixing the cream cheese, powdered sugar, milk and ¼ cup butter.

IX. Frost the top of each cake and layer until all 4 layers are frosted.

X. Cover and chill until ready to serve.

Nutritional Information

Calories 183, Fat 6.9g, Carbs 28.1g, Protein 2g

Serves: 3 to 4
Cooking Time: 15 to 20 minutes

Ingredients

½ cup maple syrup
2 tsp Worcestershire sauce
1 tsp hot pepper sauce
1 ½ to 2 lbs ribs, country style

Directions

I.   Preheat the grill to a medium-high heat.
II.   Mix the marinade by combining the sauces and syrup, make sure they are well blended.
III.   Grill the ribs for about 15 to 20 minutes, baste every few minutes after you see most of the pink is gone from the meat. Don't add the sauce too soon or you won't know if the meat is cooked thoroughly.
IV.   Once the ribs are basted, cook for another 10 to 15 minutes. Do not baste during the last 5 minutes.

Nutritional Information

Calories 188, Fat 9.4g, Carbs 2.3g, Protein 22.3g

Serves: 4
Cooking Time: 2 hours 10 minutes

Ingredients

- 1/4 cup sugar
- 2 tbsp cornstarch
- 1/8 tsp salt
- 1 banana, ripe and mashed
- 3 egg yolks, whisked
- 1/2 tsp vanilla
- 1 1/2 cup milk

Directions

I.   Combine the ingredients in a small saucepan. Whisk in the milk as the last ingredient and add it slowly.
II.   Once it boils, allow it to thicken and continue to whisk.
III.   After it has completely set, go ahead and spoon into serving bowls.
IV.   Let it chill for about an hour.
V.   Serve chilled.

Nutritional Information

Calories 185, Fat 1.4g, Carbs 42.7g, Protein 10.7g

Made in the USA
Coppell, TX
01 August 2022

80737234R00017